Ways into Technology

Building Houses

Written by Richard & Louise Spilsbury

W
FRANKLIN WATTS
LONDON • SYDNEY

First published in 2008 by Franklin Watts
338 Euston Road
London NW1 3BH

Franklin Watts Australia
Level 17/207 Kent Street
Sydney NSW 2000

Editor: Julia Bird
Design: Shobha Mucha
Photography: Paul Bricknell (unless
otherwise credited)
Artwork: John Alston
Consultant: Pam Bolton, design and technology consultant

A CIP catalogue record for this book
is available from the British Library

ISBN 978 0 7496 8082 4

Dewey Classification 690'.8

Printed in China

Picture credits:
Cover: left: Shutterstock © Bill McKelvie; middle: istockphoto © Bob
Drapella; right: Shutterstock © Alexey Fateev; p.6 (top): istockphoto ©
Owen Price (bottom) Shutterstock © Remi Cauzid; p.7 (top): istockphoto
© Michael Chen; (bottom) Shutterstock © Brad Sauter; p.8 (top): © Chris
Fairclough; (bottom) © Steve; p.9: Shutterstock © Grynka; p13:
Shutterstock © Lorraine Kourafas; p.16 (top): istockphoto © Owen Price;
(bottom) Shutterstock © Jeff Gynane; p.17 (clockwise from top right)
istockphoto: © Christine Glade; Shutterstock © Alexsander Bochenek;
Shutterstock © Christophe Villedieu; © Shutterstock © Roman Sika; p.20
(top): © Chris Fairclough; (bottom): Shutterstock © Digitalife.

Every attempt has been made to clear copyright. Should there be any
inadvertent omission please apply to the publisher for rectification.

Thanks to our models: Simran Garcha, Curtis Johnson,
Finton Reilly and Charlie Rushton.

Franklin Watts is a division of Hachette Children's Books,
an Hachette Livre UK company.
www.hachettelivre.co.uk

Contents

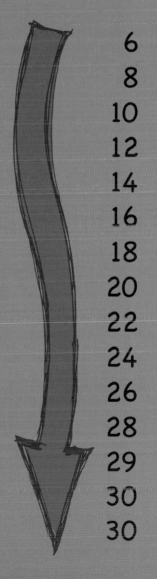

Houses and homes

People live in different kinds of homes around the world.

These are terraced houses in England.

In Mongolia, some people live in these tents called gers. Gers fold up so people can move around easily.

In Kerala in India, some people live on houseboats like these.

Inside this American apartment block there are many floors and hundreds of homes!

Why do we need homes? What other kinds of home can you think of?

Building a house

Builders make the foundations of a house first. Foundations are the base of a house. They make it stable.

Walls hold up the roof and form the sides of the rooms inside. What will go in this gap?

Doors open and close so we can get in and out. Why do windows open?

The roof keeps the inside of the house dry. What do the parts of this house do?

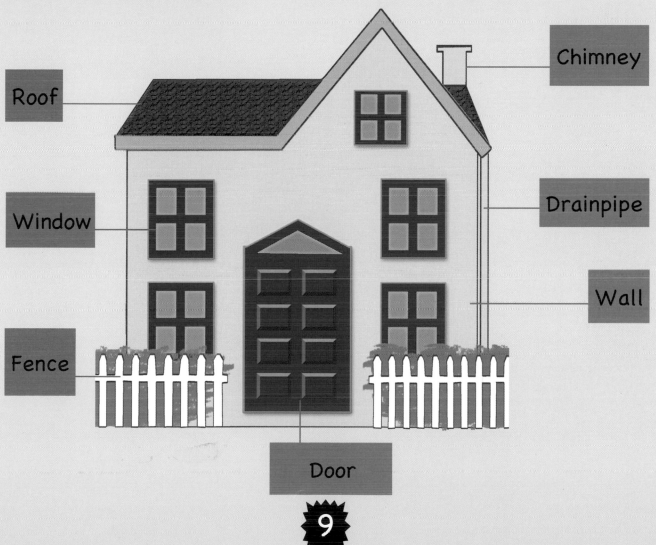

Roof

Chimney

Window

Drainpipe

Wall

Fence

Door

9

Make a **brick** house

Charlie is building
a house out of
plastic bricks.

He overlaps the
bricks to make
strong walls.
A wide base will
help to make the
house stable.

Charlie measures the side of the house.

He cuts a piece of card that is half as long again as the side to make a roof.

Charlie folds the card to make a pointed roof. He attaches it to the house with blobs of Plasticine.

How else could Charlie attach the roof to the house?

Shapes and symmetry

This picture uses different shapes to make a house.

Triangle

Square

Circle

Rectangle

What colour are the circles?
How many circles are there?

What shape is the roof?

Can you make a house with shapes?

Something is symmetrical when one side is an exact reflection of the opposite side.

The front of this house is symmetrical.

Draw one half of a house and get a friend to finish it.

Is it symmetrical?

Building a  castle

Simran is making a castle out of boxes. She uses a long tube for a tower. She makes a cone for the top.

Toolbox
- Old boxes • Scissors
- Tape • Paint • Glue

To make the windows, she draws around a box and cuts out the shape. What shape are the windows?

Simran paints
the tower grey.
She paints the
castle grey, too.

She sticks the
tower to the
castle with
glue. She makes
a door and
battlements out
of black paper.

What other
features could
Simran add?

Materials and homes

Houses are built from different materials.

This new block of flats is made from glass and concrete.

This old cottage has a thatched roof and stone walls.

Thatch

How else are old and new houses different?

Different materials have different properties.

Roof tiles are tough and waterproof.

Glass is transparent. We can see through it.

What are these house parts made from? Why?

Create a **cottage**

Curtis is making a cottage. He cuts two long rectangles of card and two short ones.

Toolbox
- Cardboard • Scissors
- Tape • Pieces of foam
- Paint • Glue • Lolly sticks

Curtis cuts out some windows and a door.

He tapes the walls together. He adds wooden lolly sticks in the joins to make the cottage stronger.

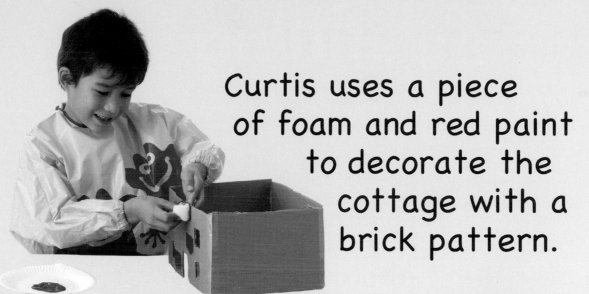

Curtis uses a piece of foam and red paint to decorate the cottage with a brick pattern.

Curtis adds a roof. He glues lolly sticks to it to make it look like thatch.

What materials could Curtis use for the windows?

Designing homes

People who design houses are called architects. They think about the size of a house, who it is for and how it will look.

Architects make scale models like this one to test their ideas. How do models help?

Architects also draw a plan
for the inside of a house.

How many
rooms does
this house
have?

Who do you think it is
designed for?

What kind of house will you design?
How many rooms will there be?

Finton designs a new bedroom for his sister. He draws a floor plan.

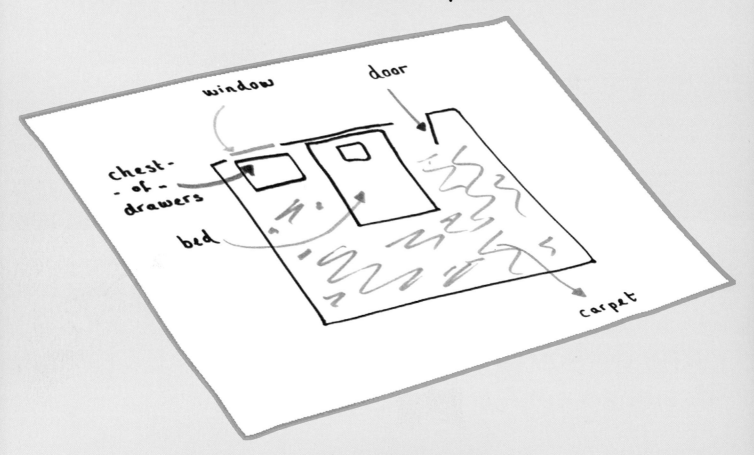

Finton is going to make the model bedroom in a cardboard box. What materials do you think he will use?

First, Finton cuts off
the front of the box
so he can see
inside it.

Next, Finton makes a door. He cuts
it out using a tool called
a paper drill and some
scissors. He sticks the
door back on with
tape. The tape
makes a hinge.

Where else could you use a hinge on a
model house? Turn the page to find out.

Make the **bedroom**

You can also make a hinge for a window.

Finton measures and cuts out fabric for a carpet and curtains.

He puts the carpet at the bottom of the box and staples the curtains above the window.

What else could he add to the bedroom?

Finton makes a bed out of a box. He uses material for a bedspread and glues on a piece of paper plate for a headboard.

Finally, he paints and glues three matchboxes together to make a chest of drawers.

What kind of room will you design and decorate?

Toolbox
- Large box • Small boxes
- Glue • Tape • Stapler
- Paper drill • Paper plate
- Scissors • Fabric and carpet scraps

This chart shows the different homes that the children in a class live in.

Which kind of house do most people live in?

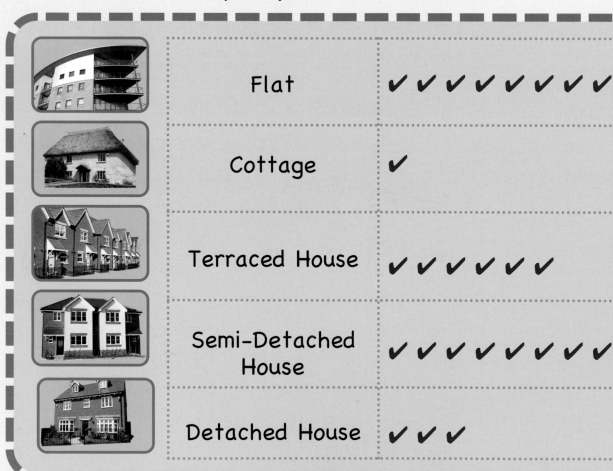

	Flat	✔✔✔✔✔✔✔
	Cottage	✔
	Terraced House	✔✔✔✔✔✔
	Semi-Detached House	✔✔✔✔✔✔✔
	Detached House	✔✔✔

Here are some photos of building materials and different house features. Can you match the features with the materials used to make them?

Glass

Bricks

Tiles

Roof

Wall

Window

Useful words

Apartment block – a building with a number of floors that is divided into many different homes.

Architect – person who designs buildings.

Battlement – a notched wall built around the tops of castles. Archers would fire arrows through the notches to defend the castle.

Chart – a way of presenting information.

Cottage – a small house, usually standing on its own, usually old and sometimes thatched.

Design – to plan something and decide what materials should be used to make it.

Features – features are the parts of something. The features of a house include the roof and windows.

Foundations – the base of a house.

Hinge – the joining point on a part like a door that allows it to open and close.

Materials – things we need to make something. Plastic, fabric, metal and wood are all materials.

Properties – the properties of a material describe what it is like. For example, glass is see-through.

Scale model – a scale model is a small version of a larger object. A model is not flat like a picture. A model has width and depth and height.

Stable – when something is stable it stands up strong and does not tip or topple over.

Symmetry – something is symmetrical if one side is an exact reflection of the opposite side.

Terraced houses – houses that are attached to other buildings on both sides.

Waterproof – when something is waterproof, it does not let water through.

28

Here are some answers to the questions we have asked in this book. Don't worry if you had some different answers to ours; you may be right, too. Talk through your answer with other people and see if you can explain why it is right.

page 7   Homes shelter us from the weather and give us somewhere to be alone or with our families. There are many other kinds of homes, such as bungalows, detached and semi-detached houses and mobile homes.

page 8   A window will go in this gap.

page 9   Windows let in light and let us see out. A roof protects a house from the weather and keeps the rain out. Fences mark the border of the garden. Chimneys let out smoke from fireplaces. Drainpipes collect rainwater and carry it away. Walls form the sides of a house and hold up the roof. Doors let us in and out of a house.

page 11   Charlie could use clear tape to attach the roof.

page 12   The circles are green. There are three circles. The roof is a triangle shape.

page 14/15 Simran's windows are rectangles. Simran could add things like a blue paper moat around the castle and a cardboard and string drawbridge.

page 16   Old and new homes are similar but often use different materials, for example, new homes often have plastic window frames and old houses can have window frames made of wood. Look at some old and new houses to see what different materials you can spot.

page 17   The door is made of wood and its handle is made of metal. The drainpipe is plastic. Wood and metal have been chosen because they are strong. Plastic has been chosen because it is waterproof.

page 19   Curtis could use tracing paper or clear plastic for the windows.

page 20   Scale models give people a better idea than a flat picture of exactly how a house will look when it is finished.

page 21   The house has eight rooms. It has three bedrooms so it is probably designed for a family.

page 24   Finton could colour the walls and stick posters or pictures to them. He could also make a cupboard and even a desk.

page 26   Most people in the class live in flats and semi-detached houses.

page 27   The roof is made from tiles. The wall is made from bricks. The window is made from glass.

Index

About this book

Ways into Technology is designed to encourage children to think about the way the things in their world are designed and made. The topic of 'Homes' is popular for this age group and an easy and familiar one for children to think and talk about.

• When looking at the parts of a house on pages 8-9 you could link back to pages 6-7 and find more pictures of houses to get the children thinking about why house features are different around the world. For example, in snowy regions sloping roofs help snow to slide off, and in coastal areas some house foundations are stilts to hold the house above the water! This gets them thinking more clearly about why we need shelters.

• Working through the book will encourage children to think about the properties of the different materials used in different parts of houses and kinds of houses. They could test the properties of materials they choose to use. For example, when choosing found materials for a structure, do they need something strong, waterproof, transparent, bendy?

• When thinking about making structures stable (see page 10) children could investigate other methods of making structures stable, such as attaching them to a firm base, using props or supports or creating a framework and sticking lighter card walls to that. They could test the stability of their structures in fun ways, such as blowing a hairdryer at them to simulate wind or resting weights on them.